shakti mhi

The Enigma of
Self-Realization

THE ENIGMA

of

SELF-REALIZATION

by
shakti mhi

1st Edition, 2007

Published by Essention Publishing,
Vancouver, British Columbia, Canada

1st Edition, 2007. First printing.

Design by Jen Eby
Enigmus concept by Daniel Mirecki
Author photograph by Nick Seiflow

Library and Archives Canada Cataloguing in Publication Data

mhi, shakti
The Enigma of Self Realization
Editors: Mary Stern and Peggy Richardson
ISBN 978-0-9784584-0-9

1. Meditation – essays.
2. Enlightenment – essays.
mhi, shakti, 1963 – . I. Title

Dewey Decimal: 291.4

Printed and bound in Canada by Friesens.
Distributed worldwide by essentionpublishing.com.

There are many layers to the symbol of the snake question mark, which we have named Enigmus. Throughout human history, the snake has been used to denote wisdom and mystery. Joseph Campbell, in the book *The Power of Myth,* explained that "...the snake is a symbol of life throwing off the past and continuing to live. The snake sheds its skin just as the moon sheds its shadow." The symbol of the snake wrapping itself around a question mark is a symbol of the inherent wisdom in all of us, where the answer is often contained within the question itself.

What often allows us to reveal the unknown and unseen is a change of perspective, a different lens; a shedding of old ways of seeing and being, the shedding of the temporal skin.

To Daniel

Contents

About this Book

The teaching in this book emerged from silence.

It has nothing to do with scriptures or holy writings.

It has nothing to do with lineage, gurus or paths.

The teaching in this book arose without
interference of the mind.

It was revealed beyond mind, beyond self,
beyond shakti mhi.

The teaching in this book belongs to the moment.

The Fifth Element

The gigantic boat was moving quietly towards the massive glacier's wall, cutting through the icy water like a sharp knife, carving a temporary scar in the big blue ocean.

The pieces of ice that had detached from the glacier were floating like giant blue lotus flowers. As we got closer to the solid frozen wall, the boat stopped moving. The sound of the main engines disappeared. I looked at the primordial, untouched nature of Alaska that surrounded us.

I realized that I was experiencing the missing element for the first time. For many years I had felt that there were more than four elements in the composition of creation. There was a fifth element that completed the four elements of earth, water, fire and air. For years, I had been yearning for the missing element, not knowing what it was, but suspecting its existence. And here I was at last, standing in the presence of utmost beauty: an enormous blue glacier with mountains, forests, sky and water all around. At last I was face to face with the missing fifth element... silence.

The silence was everywhere: in the water, in the mountains, in the air, and in me. It resonated from the glacier wall right through the atoms of my body. For the first time, I sensed the nucleus of my inner silence, of my inner being. I felt I was at home, the same home I had longed for in my youth – an indescribable longing that had brought me to the search for realization.

The silence was vibrating my soundless existence. I could recognize its melody resonating from within my meditations. I realized the whole universe is made of the essence of silence hidden beneath all sounds. The silence is built into our molecules, giving us the ability to be in stillness. When the mind takes over our existence by creating a constant inner chatter, our soundless state gets buried beneath the endless noise.

Meditation is the tunnel that takes us under the ripples of the noisy world to the soundless land, where existence manifests itself only through experience, without any interpretation of the mind.

The Four W's

Many scientists and philosophers believe that if we don't try to answer THE FOUR Ws of our existence, life has no meaning.

The questions are:
Who are we?
Where did we come from?
What should we do?
Where are we going?

The fundamental obstacle is that these questions rise up from the mind. That means they are forming from the mind's perceptions, which have nothing to do with reality as it is.

If reality happens outside of the realm of the mind, how can the mind have the tools to question it?

Imagine you are in a room that has no windows or doors, and you have never seen the outside of the room. The room is the only reality you know. You assume there is the 'outside of the room' because of the existence of the walls around you, but you have never experienced it in any way. You are curious and you wonder, what is out there? All your questions can be formed only from what you experience inside the room.

So even though you are questioning something that you don't know, your questions will be formed only from what you do know:

Are there walls outside?
How big is the outside?

What shape does it have?
Why we are inside, and not outside?
Can we get outside?
Are we inside the room for the purpose of discovering what is outside of it? Etc.

Your total experiences of the room will be the ingredients that format your questions about the unknown outside.

The question is: are any thoughts from what we already know relevant to the unknown? If the questions are wrong, how can the answers be right?

We are assuming that in the absolute reality outside of our minds, the format of question-answer exists at all.

We are assuming that in the reality outside of our perceptions, there is any reason to ask.

If no one is around when a tree falls, is there a sound? If no mind is in existence to perceive reality, are there any questions?

It is like measuring water with the speed of light because that is the only method you know. Even if you master the calculation of the speed of light, it is not relevant for the state of water.

The only way to experience reality as it is, is to experience it as a whole. The moment you are questioning, you are not a whole, as you are missing the part that you question.

What is Realization?

Realization means experiencing reality as it is in each moment and not as the mind reflects it.

As a metaphor, imagine existence as the Universe and the mind as a gigantic, sophisticated telescope. When you look at the universe through the telescope, you will always see only a part of the universe through it, no matter how refined the telescope is. The best telescope is too limited to convey the whole picture. Besides this, the image you see depends on what filter you use, the angle of the lens, the power of the magnification, and the clarity of the atmosphere.

Whatever you see through the telescope seems very real. Only when you move away from it to look directly at the universe, do you all of a sudden see the whole picture. Nothing stands between you and the experience anymore: this is not unlike realization!

It may take some time to train your vision to be less dependent on the telescope for perception.

In the same way, seeing reality through the filters of the mind will not give you the whole picture, nor will it reveal it as it is. You may see reality through the eyes of a female or a male, a bachelor or a married person, a Christian or a Buddhist, a white or a black person. All the above will affect your reality: it will be what your mind and senses experience instead of the perception of reality as it is.

The "Small Self": The Inhibitor of Realization

What stands between us and realization is the small self.

The small self is the self that identifies with the physical body and everything else that may sprout from it: physical sensations, thoughts, emotions, actions, etc.

The small self perceives existence through its own physicality and senses. As a result of seeing reality through the 'eyes' of the physical body, and the mind which perceives reality, the small self creates its own individual 'movie' in each moment that has nothing to do with reality as it is.

For example, you plan to go for a picnic but it rains. You feel upset about the rain, but at the same time a farmer, a few miles away, is happy for the rain as it helps his crop. Is rain a good or bad thing? Which of the two individuals perceive reality in its absolute?

'Small self' is the perception within us that we are separate from everything around us. 'Small self' is the illusion of personal and private experience. I am – you are, my body – your body, my country – his country, our God – their God.

The small self can also be defined as the limited self that cannot see the picture outside of itself, the totality beyond its own body, mind, thoughts and concepts.

When and How is the Small Self Formed?

From the moment we are born, we are taught that our body is who we are, that it distinguishes us from everything else. Then, we are branded with a name as a unique identification. Our names were verbalized constantly to confirm our individual existence.

When a name becomes such a significant part of our identification, it becomes very fragile because of its potential of being harmed. For most of our lives we are busy trying to protect our respective names, trying to be right, fighting for our rights, to be winners and to reach out for love and acknowledgment.

The mind is formed and programmed by all things, beings, and events around us.

The dictionary defines programming as "a set of coded instructions that enables a machine, especially a computer, to perform a desired sequence of operations."

As individuals we are programmed with a 'set of coded instructions' by parents, teachers, the media, governments and our religions, so we can 'perform a desired sequence of operations' that suits whatever system we live in.

Just as the definition of the small self sprouts from separation ('I am' as opposed to 'you are'), the small self continues to form separate definitions for everything inside and outside of it.

All definitions that describe the small self are relative.

None of your definitions as a small self exists as an absolute. You are the tallest until somebody taller stands beside you, you are the youngest until a sibling is born, and you are known until you meet somebody who doesn't know you. There is nothing absolute in those definitions of 'who' you are. This fact turns the 'small self' into a very relative concept.

The small self exists in and through separation. As a consequence, we perceive reality as a collection of polarized concepts (today / yesterday, here / there, in / out, me / you). Separation is the source of suffering for the small self.

Recognition of suffering is what drives some of us to seek different approaches to our existence. Different approaches may reveal a new and more objective reality.

The Small Self as Onion

The small self is like an onion, made up of layers of definitions of self. If you pull off all the layers, you won't find anything in the centre that will reflect your essence as a definite being. On the contrary, you may discover nothingness – you may discover that you are no one.

The small self is made of complex collections of definitions that, together, give the illusion of your existence as an 'I am'. If you check all the definitions that encompass who you are, you will find that none of them can stand on their own. They are all relative and incomplete.

Stupid people make you smart; the smarter make you stupid.

The rich make you poor, the poor make you rich.

The young make you old, the older make you young.

Your children make you a parent, your parents make you a child.

Your small self keeps changing roles relative to everything, everybody, anywhere, any time. Knowing this fact will make you wise.

The onion's layers represent the roles we fill as 'small self'. All of us keep shifting between roles. We are lovers, parents, sons, and daughters, employees, bosses, customers, servants and citizens. We change roles like we change suits. You are a teacher when you teach and a shopper when you shop.

If you hold onto the idea that you are a teacher when you pick up a milk carton from the shelf in the supermarket, you are a fool. Who are you when you sit on the toilet? Are you a banker, a doctor, a teacher, a businessman, a wife? Or maybe you are just a pooper?

Identifying with any one of your roles is like confusing the suit you wear with your own skin. When you start to identify your suit as your skin, you never take it off and wash it. It starts to stink.

Often I am introduced to people at social events. As we shake hands the person might introduce herself as Doctor so and so. What is it, in that moment when she stands in front of me sipping on her martini, that makes her a Doctor? How is the title relevant to our conversation about the selection of wines? When people start to identify with their titles they become very fragile, and as a result, defensive. They feel that if their title is erased, they will vanish as a self.

If you identify with your role as a son or daughter, who are you after your parents die? If you identify yourself with the role of being a parent, who were you before your children were born?

This is how suffering arrives. Titles, positions and roles can be destroyed. Others may not appreciate or acknowledge them. None of our roles are permanent, and in consequence, cannot represent our true essence.

Ego: The Bodyguard of the Small Self

We are all conceptual beings – a walking collection of concepts. You are;

- · Your sex
- · Your name
- · Your age
- · Your body
- · Your profession
- · Your history
- · Your character
- · Your profession, etc.

All the above may form your total identity, but none of them represent your essence – that which never changes, that which always stays the same.

All the concepts that form who you are, are changeable.

Some of you will choose the word or concept 'soul' as the essence of the self. Once you verify your description for the term 'soul', you may find that you are still very much in the realm of concepts and ideas. Good soul, bad soul, old soul, young soul, lost soul.

The ego is the bodyguard of the small self. The ego makes sure that all the definitions that make up your small self (your identity) stay glued together. Otherwise, the small self will cease. Everything that exists is prone to cease along with any of the definitions of who you are. At any given time, any and all of your definitions are at risk of being shaken by people or events that contradict your own self-definition. When this happens, your ego reacts by taking a defensive (self-protective) stance.

For instance, if you carry the definition of yourself as a great driver, and somebody cuts you off on the road, your ego reacts with anger because you have been dismissed as a driver. If at the same time the other driver makes a rude gesture, your ego reacts even more because the gesture destroys your definition of who you are as a man or woman, or the way you see yourself.

If one of your self-definitions is being slim, then merely overhearing someone using the adjective 'fat' to describe you may be enough to cause a reaction of insult, anger and frustration: all weapons of the ego.

If you have an idea of yourself as a good parent, but your teenager has a very different definition of you as a parent ("you are a horrible mother"… "you don't understand me"…), your ego will react with a variety of emotions as a result.

All these emotions arise from the ego (the self's bodyguard) to protect your self-definition.

Reactions are the manifestation of the ego's emotions in action.

When you let go of yourself as a conceptual being, nothing can hurt your 'self' anymore, and the ego as a guard fades away slowly. You shift from reacting to simply acting.

Reaction springs from your inner dialogue.

Action springs from your inner silence.

The Unsatisfied Self

Imagine taking a piece of gold and melting it into different forms of jewelry, such as earrings, a ring, a bracelet or a necklace. You show the jewelry to person A, asking him what he sees and he says, "I see earrings, a ring, a bracelet and a necklace." You show them to person B, asking him what he sees and he says "I see gold."

Person A represents the small self that sees forms and identifies with them. Person B represents the observer who sees the essence beyond the forms. After all, the ring as a form is temporary, as it can be melted to become an earring, a pendant, etc. As for the gold, its essence remains unchanged, no matter what form it takes.

Like gold, the essence of existence manifests itself in infinite forms, and your existence is one of those. Your existence as body/mind is limited, because it represents only a segment of your entire actual existence. If you are a woman, you are not a man, and if you are a human being, you are not a tree. If you are old, you are not young.

If you identify with your form you will always be lacking. You will miss the essential part of you which manifests in all the other forms that exist. You are the ocean, you are the mountains, you are the galaxies, you are she, and you are he.

As a result of feeling separated from everything that you perceive is 'not you', the small self is in a perpetual state of lacking.

The small self, as a 'separate piece of existence' can never feel complete, and constantly demands to complete its state of lacking, expressed through endless desires. "Now I feel complete." is often a statement of a self that has temporarily satisfied its sense of lack through relationships, possessions, career, consumption, entertainment, etc. It can feel 'complete' for a time, and then the desires return.

Only when we shift from the small to the higher self, immersing back into oneness, can we let go of all of our definitions (I am a woman/man, success/failure, beautiful/ugly). This is when the sense of separation and lacking ceases, and with it the sense of not being complete. In this state all desires vanish and internal peace ascends within.

Acknowledgment

It started a long time ago…when we were living in tribes in dangerous and wild surroundings, where our lives depended on other members of the tribe. To survive we needed the support of the group. Our status in the community, and the way in which we were accepted or not accepted by its members, could be crucial for our existence. The need to belong and be acknowledged by others is an evolutionary device which is encoded in each cell of our body. Our environment may have changed throughout the years, but what we are composed of remains the same. This is why the intent in most of our actions is to be acknowledged and accepted by the people around, regardless of how well we know them.

Our self-image is printed on a canvas made up of countless eyes, that reflect and perceive us in each moment. There are the eyes of our family members, friends, neighbours, partners, lovers, colleagues, the people on the street, the cashier in the supermarket, and depending on our beliefs, the ultimate eyes; those of God. If all these eyes shut, the canvas would cease to exist, and with it our self-image.

We choose careers that give us prestige, we dress to fit in or to get attention. We choose the symbols of social status and wear them (or drive them) to show others who we want them to think we are, and to be acknowledged by them.

We strive to be loved, we fulfill expectations, we make our choices by what is appropriate, we get married, and have children and much more. As a consequence we constantly worry about what others think of us. We live in a collective jail whose walls are made of dense 'recognition' material. The gates are open, but we can not leave as we are trapped in our own perception that there is no existence for the 'self' outside of the walls of recognitions. We'd rather stay in prison and keep feeding our self-image through others' eyes, than step out of our jail and let go of the self. We carry the illusion that once our self-image fades out, nothing will remain of us.

On the contrary, stepping out of the collective jail is where you will experience true freedom and meet your essence as a higher self – the imageless self.

Can you imagine an alternative existence where you do not need to get up in the morning and be sexy or desirable, young forever, or smart; you do not need to fit anymore into the standards of beauty, success, status, power, happiness, degree of education, etc.? Instead you can sink into your skin and just be. You can experience living your authentic life.

We are what the eyes of others see us to be.

Developing our own internal eyes to see reality as it is allows us to see ourselves for whom and what we really are, in our essence.

The Search for
Recognition

Take a moment, and try to recall all the people in your life whose approval and acknowledgment you have sought.

Your parents.

Your partner.

Your children.

Your friends.

Your boss, your colleagues, your employees.

The salesperson in the store.

The waiter in the restaurant.

The small self often expresses itself through the projection of other observers. We are what our parents, friends, colleagues and strangers see. Your small self is constantly formed and changed by others' perceptions of you.

When you are in a room with five other people, exactly six versions of your small self exist simultaneously and none of them are the same. Each person in the room, including yourself, perceives 'you' differently. You are the way people around you perceive you. You are the product of the others' eyes, and you are aware of it from a very young age.

The small self is like the moon that cannot see itself but is aware of its own reflection in the river below. If the river is quiet, the reflection is still. If the river is turbulent, the reflection is broken. If the river dries up, the reflection of the moon ceases. As a result of this limited self-perception, the moon fully depends on the river for its 'existence', not knowing that its reflection on the water has nothing to do with its true being.

To keep our small self alive, we need constant recognition from those whom we unknowingly choose as our creators.

We manipulate people to love us so that we are lovable. We demand respect from others to become respectable. We ask for words or deeds of appreciation so we can know that we are important. We demand loyalty to make sure our status is elevated. We reach for attention to make sure we are visible. We adapt society's codes of appearance to know that we belong. We exhaust ourselves in games of attraction so that we will know we are desirable. Like the moon, we need a river of people to acknowledge us, to be sure we exist.

Our perception of ourselves through the eyes of others creates a dependency. Through the constant search for recognition we lose our freedom to just be. We become slaves to the ones who create us as a concept.

You are talented, strong, beautiful, smart, lovable and important only when others see you in this manner. Otherwise you are nobody.

Only you can tell how much effort and energy you invest in these reflections.

Only you can tell how much of your happiness and misery depends on the feedback you get from the outside world, and how much of your actions and choices are influenced by the need to satisfy your creators.

Letting go of who you are as a concept, and merging with your higher self, will free you from living for others.

The Higher Self:
A State Beyond
All Concepts

'Higher self' is our true nature, what we are in our essence beyond mind and thoughts.

It is impossible to describe the higher self, as it is beyond all concepts. While descriptions are conceptual, they are either 'this' or 'that'. The higher self is neither 'this' nor 'that'. This is why the description of the higher self can only be illustrated from what it is not.

Because language is one of our main tools for communication, we are tied to its limitations. We can use language to understand the teaching, to describe the tools to reveal or unfold realization, but with time we have to let go of the words as we shift from understanding to 'knowing'. In the state of knowing, all questions and descriptions cease.

To start knowing the higher self, one may need to think in negation to remove all identifications of the 'small self' that stop us from realizing our true essence. "I am not this body, I am not this name; I am not this thought." But even this process can become a trap. You may switch one concept (I am this body) with another (I am not this body), falling into the illusion that you are evolving, when you are actually still holding onto a conceptual understanding of who you are, or are not, instead of experiencing 'being'.

There is a story about a Zen master who used to walk around the monastery all day saying, "I am not these hands, I am not these legs, I am not this tongue," to remind himself that he is not the small self. One day one of his more astute students who was fed up hearing his master talk all day to himself in negations, took a heavy rock and threw it on the master's big toe. The master screamed in pain as he limped on one foot. The student asked the master, "If you are not this toe, then who is screaming?"

The moment we get obsessed with any concept, and it can seem to be the most evolved or spiritual one, we are still trapped in the loop of the mind (a form of the small self) that juggles between polarities or dualities: "it is either this or that."

In a state of realization, all polarities dwell in one moment. The small self, which cannot digest such a state, will call it a paradox. For the higher self, it is what it is.

As an example of a paradox, let's assume that God is a force that has no limitations. The moment it has a limitation, the force loses its divinity. The question is: can God create a rock so heavy that God himself cannot lift it? If he cannot create such a rock, God is limited, but this is impossible by our definition of a divine being. If he can create such a rock, he or she is limited because he cannot lift it. This is again impossible by our definition of the limitless divinity.

From the point of view of the higher self, all possibilities are optional. From the point of view of the small self, everything has to make sense.

Throughout life we try to make sense of everything.

Making sense means forcing the infinite existence to fit within our limited perception. Whatever spills outside of our perception doesn't make sense to us, and as a result gets avoided by the small self. This is when we stop seeing the mystery and we focus only on the manifestation.

The True Meaning of Karma

Karma in Sanskrit means Action.

The law of Karma means the law of causation: whenever there is cause there is an effect.

There is no argument that every action has a result, it's a fact you can experience yourself. Drop an apple and something will happen, as long as you don't have any expectation of the result.

But it doesn't end here.

Swami Sivananda[1] said, "the people's own Karma brings reward and punishment."

This is where the problem starts...

True spiritual practice manifests beyond the conceptual mind. If we perceive reality within the mind's concepts, we are still trapped in the Maya[2] – the illusionary dimension.

What does good action and bad action mean? Good and bad have nothing to do with reality as it is: they are simply mind-relevant concepts, that at the end of the day have no absolute meaning, except the one which defines them in that particular moment.

1 Indian philosopher and Yoga teacher, 1887-1963, who lived the life of a Parivrajaka (wandering monk), and author of over 300 books.

2 The use of the spiritual word *Maya* means to imply the imaginary world that we create around ourselves. For more information on the Sanskrit word *Maya* and its various interpretations, please investigate the philosophies of Yoga and Hinduism.

So how can we describe any action as good or bad? Good to whom? Bad from what point of view?

True spirituality is never involved with fear or reward. If we talk about Karma in terms of punishment, we speak from fears. If we talk about Karma in terms of reward, we speak from expectation. Talking about punishment and reward make spirituality no different than religion. The use of punishment and reward is a passive-aggressive way to control the masses. So, let us discuss Karma on a higher level of knowing.

Every action and thought carries a frequency of energy. If the actions and thoughts come from the need to survive, the frequency of the action's energy will be low and dense. If it comes from experiencing reality from the higher self, as being in union with everything around us, the frequency will be high.

Low frequency energy leads to low consciousness, and experiencing reality with limited perception. High frequency energy leads to high consciousness: seeing reality as it truly is.

Can You Dance Gracefully?

The mind perceives reality through dualism alone. Symbolically, this happens when we see reality through our physical eyes. The eyes convert reality in each moment to polarities, and feed the mind with the by-product. That is the way the mind consumes the total reality, concept by concept. One eye sees the day and the other eye sees the night; one eye sees man and the other sees woman. Each eye can only capture one side of the whole spectrum. As we move through life we juggle between the opposing information that the mind receives through our dual eyes. In each moment we try to identify which of the two polarities will serve our survivor existence the best. At the end of the day all the polarities we perceive fall between two main extremes; good and bad, and always from the point of view of the self.

On the contrary, the third eye is the symbol for the state in which we see the whole spectrum of reality outside of the physical eyes' dissolution. As we do so, we shift from seeing through 'two eyes', to seeing from 'one eye'. The third eye unites all polarities into oneness. We transform the one seeing into the absolute observer. This is when the constant juggle between good and bad comes to an end, and is replaced by inner stillness.

In the state of oneness the night is not separate from the day. The night withholds the day, until it delivers it in completion, at which time the day turns to be the armor of the night.

Often, seekers get confused about how to walk through daily life with oneness, while everything around manifests through polarities. *It may be all one but I am still a woman, or, the food is too hot.* Sometimes the gap between the two perceptions is so wide, that the seeker may start to experience a split personality between what he sees and what he knows.

It is like experiencing two dimensions in one moment. If someone calls me by my name, I reply to it, as it is a practical communication device among people. In the polarity perception there is me, and there is you. At the same time, I know that my name is not what I am. Therefore, if you criticize my name it won't hurt 'me', as I am not it. In this way you keep moving between the two dimensions of existence, acting in the conceptual world within the manner of oneness. In the beginning of the practice, the motion between the two states can be awkward. You may even stumble. I know I am not a woman in my essence, so can I be in a relationship or not? Am I no longer being spiritual if I take on the role of the woman in a relationship?

On the contrary, some seekers so identify with their higher self that this becomes another concept. They cannot perceive concepts anymore. They may forget to feed their body because they are not the body etc.

The art of spirituality is to act in the conceptual world with the attitude of oneness. You move from one conceptual role to the other but never identify with either.

When you learn a new dance, you may move awkwardly between the new motions. With practice, the transition from one movement to the other becomes smoother and smoother, until all you feel is one motion. The mind, which had created distractions and awkwardness by analyzing the steps, ceases, allowing your true flow to take over.

It is the same with spirituality. First you need to expand your awareness to understand the two realities; the conceptual reality created by the mind, and the unified reality as perceived by the higher self. Then you start learning to maneuver gracefully between the two until you realize the two dimensions are of one existence. It is all about grace.

You Are Nobody

On the pathless path of realization the 'aim' is to become 'nobody', so you can be anything in each moment.

In western culture it is the opposite. The goal is to be somebody.

The first question addressed to us as children when we are 3.5 feet high is, "What would you like to be when you grow up?"

This is not even the worst. Often the adults around you notify you that you are going to be a lawyer like daddy, a mother like mommy, a leader of the tribe or some other generic, predictable aspiration.

Occasionally the verdict is even harsher. You are told that *"You are a loser and nothing will become of you. You will be a 'nobody'."*

Striving to be a 'somebody' is a path towards potential suffering.

The moment you are 'somebody' you can be destroyed as a 'self' at any moment. When you are 'nobody', there is no 'body' to destroy. You are untouchable.

In the West the most insulting thing to say is, "You are nobody." In the East it means you are Buddha, the symbol of completion. How can you be complete if you are somebody or something? If you are 'this' you are not 'that'. If you miss any 'that's, you are therefore incomplete.

By being nobody you experience true freedom to become everything and anything in each moment.

As a teacher, I often meet distressed young people telling me, "I have no idea what I want to be." They sense that if they have no clear idea of what they want to be, then their bright star, in the form of a 'self', will collapse from the gravity of society into a black hole in the galaxy of existence, where nobody will be able to notice them. What they don't know is that, even though they may see themselves as a black hole, as being nobody, they hold the light within themselves. Later this will attract all the floating stars around them. The other stars will be swallowed by their formerly hidden, powerful light.

Intuition, the Voice of the Higher Self

The brain is the instrument through which reality reveals itself. Perceiving reality only through our self-identification requires the use of a very limited part of our brain. All we utilize are the parts in the brain that help us to form the self that is our identity.

For example, "I am an artist, but I am very weak in financial analysis" is an identification that will cause you to use the right half of the brain much more than the left half.

When we move away from our limited self-identification, we open a wider window to our brain, and activate larger parts of it. This process of expanding the use of our brain may lead us to experience phenomena that are perceived as unusual, like knowing about events and actions before they unfold, commonly known as intuition.

The answers to the unknown lie in the 90 percent of the brain that we don't use.

Through the practice of meditation we exploit a larger portion of the unused brain. The end of this development process is when the mind realizes itself.

If we utilize the full potential of our brains, we can expand our perception to its maximum. This is when we start to see reality as it is, beyond time and space. This state gives us the power to know, even before we process any empirical information. This is what intuition is! We tap into a spontaneous flow of events beyond logical reasoning.

Intuition and Insight

Imagine you are living in a huge mansion, so huge that you don't really know the exact size, or how many rooms it holds.

The mansion has no windows. The entrance is just one glass door. This is also the only source of light, and light only reaches the front hall. The rest of the mansion is dark. Obviously you will use the foyer as your living space. You are familiar with the space and its dark corners.

This foyer represents your identity. The familiar collection of furniture in the foyer, that you feel comfortable with, symbolizes the collection of concepts that form your small self: your name, your age, your principles, your experience and so on.

Next to the foyer there is a room that cannot be seen in the darkness. Once in a while a beam of light comes through the glass door and illuminates this room. In this flash you have a view of its contents.

This room stores moments that contain the three dimensions of time — past, present and future — as one manifestation. As a result, you can see into one moment's un-manifested potential action.

All moments hold within themselves, actions that have not been manifested yet. These actions are in potential form: capable of being, but not yet in existence.

Most people see actions only when manifested, but the eyes of those who have reached realization will see all actions in their potential form.

You might experience this insight when you hear the phone ring. You might know who is on the other end before you pick it up. Briefly, knowing the result of actions before they eventuate is intuition.

Déjà vu can be another form of transcending the usual rules of time, space and perception. Déjà vu means observing the same action unfold in different periods of time or dimensions in one moment.

Let's go back to our metaphor of the mansion. Not many people live in their mansion with an open door. They are concerned with safety. The few who feel secure enough to keep the door wide open may experience a strong ray of light entering through the open door. It may illuminate the rest of the mansion. The light may reveal that there are no walls separating the different chambers that we assume exist. Light reveals one open space that stores the treasure of existence beyond time, space and forms.

In this open space you may find your death as a present moment, or find yourself before your parents were born, before you even had a face. You may find your eternal existence in diverse but temporary forms.

No more darkness envelops your existence in this space; no more walls exist between you and reality. You are free to move.

The profound experience of insight may happen once in a while to people who keep the doors of their dwellings closed, who live their lives without light. A sudden opening of the door may be caused by a turbulent wind (a life crisis, a natural disaster) or by an unexpected guest (or a teacher) who knocks on the door.

Mass Consciousness

Do not fall into the illusion that you need to gain any special wisdom to reach enlightenment.

Antoine Lavoisier, 'the father of modern chemistry' proved that mass never changes when matter is transformed from one state (like water) to another (like steam). This is applicable to consciousness as well. Consciousness doesn't change its 'quantity' when we transform from ignorance to realization.

We are complete in terms of our consciousness's 'mass' or quantity. We cannot gain more consciousness, but we can gain more use of its capacity. It is a matter of tuning it to the finest manifestations of its absolute capacity.

In the state of realization, consciousness unifies all forms. It has the properties of a liquid because it flows spontaneously. It has the properties of a gas because it is invisible to the physical eyes, and it has the properties of a solid because it can be manifested into reality.

Life as a Movie

People who have faced death often report that at the moment they thought they were going to die, their whole life flashed before their eyes. They saw their lives like a movie, sometimes with scenes or moments they didn't even remember. Watching the movie of our lives running on our internal screens can also happen when we experience the death of the small self while we are fully alive. You may be in a silent retreat, on vacation away from your daily busy life, or just sitting in your comfy armchair watching the rain in silence, when suddenly a river of memories gushes inside you flooding you with old moments, feelings, smells, tastes and emotions.

Some of the memories may be from insignificant moments from your far past, or even all the way to early childhood, that you never even knew you were storing in your hidden warehouse. Your Granny serves you hot apple pie in the kitchen and talks to the neighbour's wife, as you watch her wide swollen ankles with wonder. Or you are 6 years old with a high fever, your mom is beside your bed with her palm on your forehead, and you don't share with her that you are afraid to die.

As you watch your life movie it seems that the motion pictures pop up randomly with different moments, at different times, and in different spaces. You are amazed by the real sense of feeling and emotions that wash over you as though it had just happened a moment ago.

The process of spiritual death, while the body is fully alive, may be called rebirth[1].

Experiencing such an event can be very significant to your spiritual evolution. In this instant you walk out of your own movie, you step out of the 2-dimensional screen that your life was playing on, and you take a seat in your private theater, watching your life in motion pictures. It is significant because you are instantly upgraded from being an actor following a script, fully identified with your role, to being a spectator, enjoying the show from your V.I.P box seat.

Watching your own movie as an observer is a great time for contemplation. As you observe your motion throughout the scenes of your life, watch your intentions, your aims, your drives, and your motives without judging them. Carefully notice the 'self' that you are identified with as an actor, and ask yourself if you are really living your own authentic life, or simply fulfilling others' expectations, moving with the momentum of life with no choice, selling your soul for false stability, safety, recognition and acknowledgment.

---

1 Do not confuse the spiritual rebirth with the therapeutic technique called rebirthing.

All this time you are sitting in the seat of the observer watching your own movie with your new interpretation. If you look behind you, you will notice a different chair with your name on it – it is for you to move into if you choose; the seat of the Director. From this seat not only can you observe the movie, you can actually direct the script you hold in your hand with your own creativity. Now the range of choice is much wider and you are much more in control of your own movie. You may sit on this chair for a while until hopefully you will be introduced to an even greater seat in the balcony of the theater; the seat of the Producer. This is the seat of power, as from it you are both the Observer and the Director, but beyond that you become the 'Manifestor'. You have the access and the source to infinite possibilities. From the moment you step out from the 2-dimensional movie screen shifting to the different power seats in the theater, you actually experience rebirth, as each time you die to your previous lower consciousness in your living physical body.

Often on the spiritual path, when the master recognizes the rebirth of his student to a higher consciousness, he gives his student a new name, as the old one symbolized the old limited role he played in the so-called movie named Maya.

Feelings and Emotions

Feelings are our intuitive sense of being in alignment with existence.

Emotions are feelings that are processed through our perceptual mind.

When feelings remain beyond the influences of the physical structure and mind they are beyond reasoning.

Emotions are sculpted by culture, upbringing, moral codes, education, social programming and biochemistry (hormones, ph levels, etc.).

Emotions are like microchips that have been planted in you to release ongoing triggers that maneuver your behavior to serve your tribe.

If you are not aware of this device, you will identify with your emotions, and as a result be fully controlled and manipulated by them.

You do not own your emotions. They own you.

Emotions form to lead us to fulfill a role in the tribe. The tribe in our ancient history was the incubator for the development of the human race. This is how emotions lead us to fulfill our evolutionary roles.

If you feel love you will mate.

If you feel jealous you won't leave your partner, and you will stay around to help take care of the offspring.

If you feel longing you will always return to your partner and tribe to help with survival.

If you feel guilty you will stay in the tribe to fight for territory.

If you feel shame you won't do things that can hurt the tribe.

If you feel angry you will react to protect your offspring and your tribe.

If you feel lonely you will stay close to the tribe for your own protection.

Because emotions envelop you to make you a great evolutionary soldier, they often sway you from your true feelings.

You may feel you want to become an artist, but your guilt towards your parents – who have certain expectations of you – will drive you to study law.

Emotions keep us in line with evolution, and take us away from our true nature as a higher self. This higher self may contradict evolution by "not serving a purpose".

For that reason alone, emotions must be a driving,

powerful force.

Emotions are so powerful that they can make us sick to death or powerfully healthy.

They can make us blind while our eyes are wide open.

Emotions can consume you in a way that will surprise and even shock you. Jealousy, for instance, can drive you into behaviour that you may not have known you were capable of.

Throughout history, individuals, cultures, religions and nations have always, and still do to this day, empower emotions and turn them into tools of manipulation.

Be Careful of Beliefs

Where experience is absent, belief and faith take over. Faith and beliefs form the 'religion placebo' for the spiritual experience.

When there is no experience, there is lacking.

Lacking creates curiosity about the missing experience.

Curiosity gives birth to questions.

Questions raise assumptions.

Assumptions that best serve our needs and fears turn into our beliefs.

Beliefs are stagnant and contrary to our spiritual evolution, and move us away from the experience.

When you experience you know.

When you don't know you believe.

Why is it that you *know* you have 2 arms but when it comes to God or to love you *believe* in it?

Frog into Prince

In the process of meditation you increase the frequency of your consciousness. At the highest frequency you have the capacity to perceive existence beyond the density of matter.

In the realm of spirituality, frequency represents the rate of energy's vibration. The lower the frequency, the denser the energy becomes. This is the nature of physical matter. As the frequency increases, the energy becomes lighter and more formless.

Everything in existence falls between the two extremes of high and low frequencies.

A rock has a low frequency and a high density. Light has a high frequency and a low density.

Even emotions have frequencies. Hate, anger and jealousy have lower frequencies. Love, joy and bliss have higher frequencies.

All low frequencies contain the potential to transform into higher frequencies and vice versa. This hidden potential of transformation is rooted in our subconscious, and is often represented as metaphors in timeless myths and legends.

For example, in the Bible, Moses witnessed the power of God (the higher self) in the transformation of a walking stick (lower frequency) to a snake (higher frequency).

We all know the fairytale about the frog who turned into a handsome prince. This is the great metaphor of the same kind of transformation.

In this tale it happens as the result of a kiss, a loving kiss. Here we have a hint that love, the highest form of frequency, is the most powerful tool for transformation.

Pinocchio's story is another metaphor for shifting to a higher frequency of consciousness. This is demonstrated when he finally ceases to be a marionette, and becomes a boy through the love of his creator.

In mythical and biblical stories, we come across descriptions of reverse transformations. In the story of Sodom and Gomorrah, when God turns Lot's wife into a pillar of salt, he demonstrates a reverse transformation from a high frequency to a lower one.

When the transformation is in reverse, it carries a negative connotation, and is often represented as punishment.

The alchemist searches for the way to transform lead, a low frequency metal, to gold, a high frequency metal.

In the alchemy of spirituality, we are changing the low frequency of ignorance (in the form of the small self) to the highest frequency of realization (in the formless higher self).

Often low frequency attracts low frequency (negative thoughts attract negative manifestations) and vice versa.

When a lower frequency is attracted to a higher frequency, like in the case of a student following a spiritual teacher, it shows that the lower frequency form, in this case, the student, is ready and open for a transition to a higher state.

Death.

The physical body is a low frequency, high-density form. The consciousness in the body is a high frequency.

In most spiritual and religious practices it is stated that although the body is mortal, the spirit (in spiritual terms – consciousness) is immortal. What this means is that when the low frequency body returns to the elements, it sets the higher frequency spirit free, which had dwelled within.

In this transformation the high frequency spirit or consciousness shifts to vibrate in a formless dimension invisible to the physical eye, like a butterfly being released from the low frequency cocoon. The death of the cocoon is the birth of the butterfly.

If we would perceive our death as a transformation to a higher frequency, not only would we not fear it anymore, we might even embrace it as a pure spiritual transition, and prepare ourselves to arrive at this powerful transitory moment with full awareness and a peaceful mind.

The Hidden Lake

Imagine a secret and infinite lake. The water is so clear that if you look down to the bottom, you can see to the centre of the universe. The surface is so still that you can see the whole of existence reflected on the water. It's been some time since you've heard about the existence of this hidden lake, and its powerful effect on those who dive into its celestial water. In this lake's depths, time and space come to an end.

And here you finally find yourself, standing on the shore, gazing at the serene lake, but hesitating to step in. You have already learned from others that to step into its water you need first to strip off everything that is not what you are. Otherwise, the majestic water will heavily soak the layers of your false identities and you may drown. Entering the lake requires nakedness inside and out. Being naked is not something that you are used to, because from the moment you were born, you were dressed up with your name and other fabrics of identities or selves. You were dressed up to protect you from the chilling fear of being a 'nobody'.

As you look through the clear water you notice that after the first step, there is no solid ground to stand on. All your life you have been used to standing on ground that gave you the illusion of being safe. The ground you are used to represents directions, goals, order and security.

For years now you have formed foundations of solid ground for your feet to walk on. You have bought houses, created a family, established your status and formed principles. You are so familiar with the ground, that in the mornings when you stretch your feet out of bed, there is no need to open your eyes. They remain sealed in your state of permanent sleep. And now, as you look at the bottomless lake, the fear of losing the familiar ground under your feet crawls into your consciousness.

It is hard for you to believe that feeling safe has nothing to do with having tangible ground under your feet. There are very few people around the lake. Some are stepping in, letting the water cover only their ankles; their eyes wide open, unfamiliar feelings flooding their senses.

Fewer still are those who immerse their whole bodies in the soundless ripples, taking in the experience of floating in an unfamiliar dimension of lightness. Amongst those on the shore contemplating their immersion, you notice powerful beings with radiant eyes walking quietly, whispering the unfolding truth: "Only by diving in will you know…" People call them the 'The Awakeners'.

Their role is to awaken the inner knowledge: that you do not need to keep your head above the surface to survive.

Some of the Awakeners energetically remove uncertainties from the would-be swimmers. Some allow new swimmers to lean on them until they become familiar with their new body mass, floating in infinity. It takes courage to dive into the unknown, but once you trust and dive in, you will never be able to say where you end and where the water begins.

A Night of Fireworks

It was late at night and the fireworks exploded in the air like miniature atomic bombs, entertaining the thousands of people who had gathered on the sea wall to celebrate togetherness.

As most people out there know subconsciously, togetherness is just a temporary panacea for loneliness, the root or knowledge of which becomes a good reason to proceed to drown the revelation in alcohol.

That night I was sitting in my urban cave watching my body manifest its deepest sense of loneliness in the form of heavy, dense pain. It felt like my whole body had become the ultimate transistor for all human suffering.

A knot in my tummy was expanding in the shape of a vortex, hardening my internal organs into cold marble. My upper back and shoulder muscles went into deep spasms, as my whole body became completely frozen. I was shattered, feeling the flow of life drain from my physical body. I couldn't move. For 50 minutes I was overwhelmed by emotion, facing the vast void of my existence as a small self.

In the midst of these emotions I compared my terrifying experience with the endless moments of deep loneliness and pain I experienced in the early years of my life. Even though that night of the illuminated sky was the most painful time of my whole existence, somehow it was different from all the other dark moments I had gone through as a young and confused woman.

Although my physical body went completely numb, my psyche was at its utmost state of alertness. With clear eyes I could see the difference between my past suffering and this present significant moment. Unlike the far past, when I had fully identified with my pain, that night, as the lights competed with the sounds in the dark atmosphere, I observed the pain cutting the flesh of my body, like a sailor watching his boat tremble in stormy water.

It had nothing to do with me. The pain just manifested itself through my body. The pain I was watching wasn't my personal pain. I was experiencing the collective pain of humanity. I was like a giant antenna transmitting the ultimate state of loneliness that human beings can possibly experience, when they manifest existence through the small self. This deep sense of loneliness emerges from the sense of being separate from everything around us. As I watched the tremendous pain move through my veins and arteries, spreading throughout my cells like terminal cancer, for the first time I truly understood why people get drunk, immerse themselves in drugs, commit suicide or become obsessed with religion or sex.

This often happens when people realize that nothing in existence is reliable as a permanent salvation. If everything is temporary, how can anything be a permanent rescue to our inner sense of loneliness and feelings of not being safe?

No man or woman out there is powerful enough to protect us from the unknown. No strong belief or knowledge can stop our physical deterioration. No abundance of material possessions or gain of status can permanently remove our sense of being fragile.

The only way to emerge from our eternal internal feeling of loneliness is by unifying with all of our other reflections.

Perfect As It Is

When I state in discourses or public talks that everything is perfect as it is, some people in the room will jump up with clenched fists and frustration in their eyes, wondering how I can say such a thing. They usually give me an example or two of terrifying and horrible things that humans can do or go through (tsunami, killing, diseases etc.), asking me if I will still call it perfect as it is.

For most of us the term 'perfect' has a positive connotation. It is a good thing. So when you evaluate a bad thing like killing with a positive term like perfection you create a paradox for the mind. Well, let's first check what the meaning of the word perfect is.

From the Oxford dictionary;

> Perfect:
>
> 1: Having all the required elements or qualities
> 2: Free from any flaw
> 3: Complete

Most people will agree with the above definition, but the problem is not the dictionary definition: the problem is from what point of view the definition is interpreted.

So for our discussion, 'perfect as it is' means that complete circumstances, with no flow, which had all the required elements that were needed for an event to occur, arose to manifest the end result. Once the action or event has already occurred, it is 'perfect as it is'. Otherwise, if anything were missing it wouldn't have manifested as it did. It is neither good nor bad: it is what it is.

For example: War is 'perfect as it is' otherwise it wouldn't happen. You may in the future, try to avoid this kind of circumstance because it doesn't serve you, but once it happens, it is as perfect as any other manifestation that has already materialized to be.

Most people perceive perfection not as an objective matter. They regard perfection as a state or quality that serves their senses, or concerns the best.

So we can say, from the 'small self' perception, that perfection is always relative. It becomes 'perfect' or 'not perfect' by the small self evaluation that is driven from its need to be satisfied. "It was perfect; it was exactly what I needed." Or, "It wasn't as perfect as it could have been, because I was too tired."

You may say that a tsunami can not be considered a 'perfect' event, as it brought destruction. What you mean is that the tsunami was bad for us. In its manifestation lay its perfection. The small self interprets and evaluates the event from its own limited point of view.

Perfection from the point of view of the ultimate observer is always an absolute. Once the perfect conditions to the perfect event arise, the event will occur in its utmost perfection.

Questions and Answers

What follows are shakti's replies to questions
from students at a meditation retreat,
Spring 2005

Does realization exist?

The debate about enlightenment's existence or nonexistence is on. It always was and always will be.

The reason for this is that once enlightenment is discussed, it naturally gets squeezed into concepts and definitions.

Definitions and concepts are the blossoming of perceptions. Perceptions are the seeds of the mind. Taking into consideration that each of our minds changes momentarily, I am leaving to you the calculation of how many spiritual minds are out there, to form countless perceptions that portray infinite definitions about enlightenment. No wonder so many spiritual seekers are in confusion, doubt and despair about the issue.

UG Krishnamurti[1] declared that there is no such a thing as enlightenment, and did it in the most enlightened manner.

J Krishnamurti[2] kept intellectualizing enlightenment, while he may have never experienced this state, or even had a glimpse of its essence.

I prefer to use the term realization instead of enlightenment.

1 Indian philosopher and spiritual teacher, b. 1918 – d. 2007. Author of several books, including *The Mystique of Enlightenment, Mind is a Myth, Thought is Your Enemy,* and *The Sage and the Housewife.*

2 Indian philosopher and spiritual teacher, b. 1929 – d. 1986. Author of several books, including *Think on These Things, Education and the Significance of Life, The Awakening of Intelligence,* and *The First and Last Freedom.*

Enlightenment sounds more like a final 'prize' that you receive as a reward, for doing the right thing. Realization can be an ongoing process towards a 'state' that in its essence manifests as 'an effortless course of actions'.

Once you reach this state of realization, it ceases to exist as describable, and remains only in the eyes watching the realized one.

So what is realization?

I cannot say…
But, if I could say…
I would say…

Realization is the ability to manifest in our full capacity.

Nobody can measure, define, describe or teach this sheer capacity of manifestation. However, some of us may experience it.

In the experience you may realize that reality is not a fixed thing.

In the experience you may realize that obstacles end when the perception of obstacles is removed.

In the experience you may realize the ability to experience the moment outside of your biology and social programming.

In the experience you may realize how to avoid

limiting the scene to the size and quality of the viewer's lens.

Realization.

You cannot gain it, as it is not outside of you. You cannot hold onto it, as it is not inside of you.

Like a shining star, collapsing into itself creating a powerful black hole and in this state of nonexistence, manifesting immense gravitational power, the same is true with realization. Describing it will make it vanish, but its void will be so powerful that it will make its seekers willing to do anything to get it.

Take it or leave it!

*I've been searching for realization
for quite a long time,
but with no success.
What could be the reasons?
Where can I find realization?*

Many people perceive realization as something that you reach out to get. They seek realization outside of themselves.

A Zen story tells about a seeker who traveled on his horse for many days through many countries, through mountains and valleys, to meet with a renowned master.

Upon arriving at the isolated cave of the master, he got off his horse and knocked on the wooden door. The old master answered the door, asking the seeker what he wanted.

The traveler answered, "I am looking for realization."

The master asked, "Why are you not looking for a horse?"

The man looked at the master with surprise and replied irritably, "Why do I need to look for a horse, when I already have one?" The master smiled softly and turned back to his cave, closing the door.

What a waste of time it is, to reach out for something when it is what you have and are already. It is not about getting realization: it is about revealing it.

Some people perceive realization as a final destination that you arrive at. From this point of view comes the term 'the path to realization'.

They imagine a path with road signs directing the

spiritual travelers to the desirable destination. The directions might be something like, "Take the Inner Peace Highway and keep going for 80 mindful breaths, then turn left to Let-Go Boulevard, and keep going for about 100 mantras until you see a gas station in the shape of a lotus. Stop there, and fuel your vehicle with prana[1], get a crystal or two in the convenience store, before you continue towards the Fifth Chakra avenue…" etc.

The fact is that there is no path to realization. There is no path, period. Every time you place your foot on the ground, *you create your own path.*

This is the reason why, when I talk about realization, I talk about the non-path of realization, or the "pathless path".

Realization is neither a destination nor something you obtain. Realization is a state of existence that you can tap in and out of. The aim is to dwell eventually in this state in each and every moment, but there is no guarantee that once you become it you will not lose it.

---

1 Prana is sanskrit for "life force".

Since departing on the spiritual path,
I often feel confusion, and even panic.
What is your advice?

Imagine the higher self (your essence) as a mother and your small self (the sense of 'I am') as an embryo.

For nine months a woman and her embryo exist as one. In the moment of separation, what we call birth, a sharp pain takes over all sensations, and brings the awareness of the mother to the moment.

Right now you are in the painful labour of birth.

For most of your life you identified with the small self as being who you were. Now you are experiencing the separation of the higher self from the small self.

When the full separation takes place and the baby comes out, the mother starts observing the baby, knowing she is not the baby anymore. The baby is part of her, but not her. From this point on she will watch the baby, take care of the baby, learn to know her baby, accept his limitations, restrain him and train him to manage reality.

In the same way, when you stop identifying with your small self, you start observing your body, mind and ego, knowing they are part of you but not who you are. Through the process of meditation you observe your small self learning, like a mother watching her baby. You accept its limitations and you master them, so that the mind won't take over.

Through the process of identifying with the higher self you become the ultimate observer. The small self becomes the observed. Naturally, the observed is always weaker in relation to the observer. The 'small self' starts losing its power as master.

Knowing this, the small self becomes like a rebellious teenager questioning his mother.

In resisting the loss of its power, the small self debates the existence of the higher self and doubts the state of realization. This is a very common state on the pathless path of realization.

As we keep shifting back and forth from the higher self (the ultimate observer), to the limited small self (the mind), we often experience a 'split personality'. This can turn into a very confusing state, into a feeling that we are losing our mind.

The more we dwell in the state of the higher self, the more peaceful we are. When your mind panics, watch it and breathe mindfully, knowing it is not you who is panicking. It is your mind.

When a small child is screaming and yelling angrily, his mother may be confused and embarrassed by his behavior, if she identifies the child's behavior as defining who she is. But if she is wise enough to know that he is just a child and she doesn't identify with his behavior as a reflection of who she is, she will deal with him much more wisely. This is how we should be relating to our screaming mind.

What exactly is meditation?

Meditation is the practice of being in the moment.

The mind suspends us between past and future. While we meditate, the experience of being in the moment occurs outside of the mind.

The stillness of meditation is the bridge that takes us outside of the mind, so we can observe it instead of being it.

Perhaps, like many people, you confuse various techniques for self-relaxation with meditation. Even though you may experience relaxation as a side effect of being in the moment, this is not the subject of meditation.

Meditation has neither subjects nor goals. Although you might have goals and subjects for meditation, and they may lead you to the practice, the transformation of being in the moment will not happen until you drop the conscious desire for meditation.

Many people think that meditation is only the technique of sitting still for a period of time. After each sitting they go back to the madness of the mind until the next appointment for sitting. Meditation means reaching for mindfulness. Mindfulness should be present throughout each moment of our existence. It should not start and end on the meditation cushion.

*I feel I am going nowhere,
wasting my time in meditation.
What can you suggest?*

Many people feel they are going nowhere with their meditation practice.

Sometimes they feel stuck.

Sometimes they feel they are not grasping the teaching.

Sometimes they feel they have 'gotten it' once, but it drifted away.

Sometimes they feel despair.

Many times they lose hope and give up the practice.

They feel that their minds are as unchanging as a rock.

Imagine a rough stone with sharp edges lying on the beach a few feet away from the water at the low tide mark. The stone has been hardened by the elements. The sun dries it, the wind sharpens it and time ages it.

From time to time when it is windy or when the ocean is stormy, the waves reach the stone, striking it with some force. At other times when the tide is high, the stone is fully immersed in the silence of the ocean, and cuddles with the moonlight that glows through the water.

The stone is the mind, the ocean is the teacher and the moonlight is the teaching.

The stone will tell you that it has nothing to do with the ocean or the moonlight. The ocean feels far away, the moonlight is high in the sky...

The stone doesn't take into account the times the water and the moon reach to it.

But in time the stone finds itself to be round, smooth and polished, shining in the sun.

Every time you sit still in meditation you polish your mind. Every time you have a moment of mindfulness, you are a step closer to manifesting realization.

Realization can unfold in one moment.

Sometimes a moment lasts for a few years.

Have patience.

Keep still.

And breathe mindfully.

In many books about meditation that I read, the mind is described as a negative force. Is this really the case, or does the mind have positive aspects as well?

Many meditators perceive the mind as a negative aspect of our existence. Many books advise us to 'kill the mind', 'destroy the mind', or something along those lines.

Do not destroy that which may be useful.

On the contrary! The mind is very important for our existence in the physical body. It serves us as a guard in survival, it is a wonderful tool for learning, it helps us to take care of our bodies and to manage protection from the elements. In the wilderness we didn't have any physical features that gave us any advantages in fighting against animals or the elements of nature. Our teeth are not strong enough to kill or eat certain food. Our nails are not strong enough to protect us or to help us climb, nor do we possess any poison within our body as a weapon. Our eyes and ears are not sharp enough for hunting. We can neither crawl under the ground nor dive to the bottom of the ocean to hide or find food, and we cannot fly if we need to escape. Relatively speaking, we are weaponless, weak creatures. To our favour, what we do possess is a powerful mind that can create, invent and learn to find solutions. So we do not want to kill or destroy this amazing valuable endowment that we've got.

If it is used in the right way, it is the greatest gift that humans have, but if it is used with ignorance, it can be a curse both for us and for the world around us.

Because the mind is a complex, sophisticated entity, it can take over our lives without us noticing.

The key question to consider is, "Do you use your mind, or are you being abused by it?"

Only you can answer that question.

Make sure that your mind doesn't answer it for you.

*Is the Higher Self
not just another concept
of the mind?*

Great question, and yes, you are right! It is another concept.

Language is a handy but very limited tool used for describing experiences authentically. Only concepts can be expressed through language.

The higher self, if not experienced, remains a concept like any other concept. I use the term 'higher self' to distinguish a state of being that cannot be perceived by the mind, and yet needs to be understood by the mind as we talk.

This is why true practice starts when words end. For this reason, allow my words to resonate in you but do not hold onto any of them. They are just the mind's by-products, and the mind is defined by its own limitations.

'Higher self' is everything that you are, and that you are not.

'Higher self' is everything inside you and outside of you.

The higher self unveils itself when all concepts cease. Concepts form in the dimension of time and space. When time and space (concepts themselves) cease, all concepts unite to be one or none. What's left is the experience, which is experienced by the higher self and is the higher self.

All concepts are polarities which are formed by time

and space; here and there, now and later, you and me, and good and bad.

If you unite all polarities, they nullify each other to become none or one. They all unite to be the infinite possibilities of manifestations that exist in one moment. This is the nature of the higher self.

All concepts are partial and incomplete because they are creations of thought. Thoughts are only broken glimpses of reality, so we never see reality as it is through the mind.

The higher self emerges when we move beyond mind and language.

To understand we need words – thoughts of the mind. For 'knowing' we need none. This is why proper teaching leads to experience and not to a philosophy, not to an interpretation, not to scriptures, not to words. It is stillness in action, beyond time, space, and thoughts.

Any description of any experience, even the most accurate, will be far from the experience itself.

Be mindful today, of those moments when you sit out in the garden watching the trees, the ocean and the wind. You may notice that by watching the ocean you use it as a background for your racing thoughts. The 'experience' is in the back of your mind. But maybe a moment will come when the ocean you are watching as a background for your thoughts will move forward to be the 'experience', and leave no space for the mind to interfere with interpretations. In that moment there is no thought, no mind, no watcher, and no watching. It is what it is – an experience. Rarely do people experience an experience. They usually 'experience' an interpretation of their moment through the mind filters.

As a result, seldom do people immerse fully into the moment: the only time that exists.

*How does Karma affect those
who know its laws?
Are they affected more than those
who are not aware of these laws?*

Karma will affect the one that believes in it. The effect will be in the form of the meaning that each person gives to it.

Let us say that as a spiritual seeker you move through life trying not to do "bad" things to avoid creating bad Karma. By doing so, you don't really care about anything outside of yourself, but only about your own good or bad Karma. So where is your spiritual evolution? You still live for your own sake. You still act like a little child who's mainly afraid to be punished. But, if you move in the world knowing and experiencing that everything around you is your reflection, you will always try to act from love. As everything is one, everything is you.

*Is it possible to love someone
without being attached to them?*

Non attachment means, 'not to hold onto'.

Detachment means 'to cut off from something'.

When you love people with no attachment, their actions never affect your love for them. You may like or dislike their actions but the love stays untouched.

Attachment arises when we reach out for love or fulfillment from a need. The subject of our love or fulfillment becomes like a crutch. Without this crutch we feel we cannot be complete. We reach to our subject with invisible hands and wrap our fingers around it, so it won't disappear. The ten fingers of the invisible hands are possession, manipulation, obsession, jealousy, expectation, fears, emotional blackmail, blame, suspicion and demand.

After an extended period of time of holding our subject of attachment tightly to us, it may seem like it is attached to us. This attachment creates heaviness as it is happening by force. Try to hold on to a feather for few days without letting go of it. Even though the feather is the proverbial benchmark of lightness, you will feel after a while that you are holding onto a heavy weight that hurts your clenched fist. Even if you hold on to lightness, it can become a heavy burden as a result of holding too tightly and not letting go.

For detachment to happen you need first to be attached. Only separate things can be attached.

When things are one, the concepts of attachment and detachment cease.

If you sense a fear of getting hurt by anything that you perceive to be attached to, you may detach yourself from it physically, emotionally or mentally for the sake of safety or defense. This detachment can be a conscious or an unconscious process, as when one responds defensively from a fear of feeling hurt or of loss.

The act of cutting yourself off creates an even deeper sense of separation and may change the quality of your 'love' all the way to become hate or any other variation in between.

Many people believe that non-attachment must go hand-in-hand with the concept of not caring. They confuse non-attachment (not holding on to) with detachment (cutting off from). Detachment is like an artificial surgery where the knife, in the shape of ignorance, cuts into oneness and separates us as a self ('I am'), from everything that we perceive as not ourselves. In the case of detachment, we may indeed not care, as the subject of our love doesn't serve us anymore.

As long as we identify with the small self as a form (body-mind-ego), we separate ourselves from everything around us that we don't perceive as part of us.

When we move beyond the form of the small self, the sense of separation vanishes. This is where the true experience of oneness takes place. In this state, we become one with all forms of existence. Once we unite with everything around us, there is nothing left not to care about, as everything is 'us'.

Can you talk about creativity?

Creativity is a pure energy that showers from the higher self, the source of everything and of nothingness.

Creativity means spontaneous creation. It is beyond logic, explanation, knowledge, aim or reasoning.

In the process of creativity the mind must be put aside to make internal space for the creative energy to burst through.

The mind cannot be the source of creativity. It can only be the instrument that manifests or expresses it. When mind is the source of creativity; when reason, aim or thoughts are involved in the process, creativity shifts to become invention[1].

When you come across true creativity as an observer, it hits the core of your being before your mind grasps it, if at all.

What makes a genius is a huge capacity that allows a high voltage of creative energy to blast through the body, mind, and brain as instruments.

In many cases, even though the capacity of body/mind may be large enough to channel the energy from the higher self, the high intensity of the energy can burn the instrument. This may cause rapid deterioration of the instrument (the physical body and mind), or it may lead to insanity.

---

1 Definition of Invention: "the creation of something in the mind", "the act of creating something by thinking" (see "Sources").

*Can you please explain
the meaning of this verse
from Tao Te Ching:*

When nothing is done,
nothing is left undone.
I do my work, then step back,
the only path to serenity.
When my work is done, I forget it,
this is why it lasts forever.

When nothing is done,
nothing is left undone.

The mind cannot perceive reality as one entity. It perceives existence through different concepts. Concepts are dualistic in nature. The moment a concept is formed, it distinguishes itself from everything it is not, creating a perception based on polarities. Night exists when day exists, beauty exists when ugliness exists, life exists where death exists, 'I' exist when others exist, etc.

Because the mind exists through dualism, it bounces from one polar concept to another, trying to complete all the incomplete perceptions. It doesn't realize that the complete and the incomplete are one; that nothing is perfect, and that is what makes it perfect as it is.

We fall into the illusory thinking that we are the doers, not realizing that we manifest the actions. We fall into the illusory idea that we are the start and the end of events, phenomena and actions, not seeing that in our essence we are part of an immeasurable infinite dynamic.

I do my work, then step back,
the only path to serenity.

When the action of doing comes into existence through you, there is no opinion of it or attitude to it, left in you. You step back with no ownership of the action or its result. When you are the 'doer', you always risk ending with results that may not suit your motivations, goals or purposes. Believing you are the doer, this may set up expectations that may end with disappointments and suffering. Serenity will arrive when you have no attachment to the actions because "they flow from the core of your being." (Tao Te Ching.)

When my work is done, I forget it
this is why it lasts forever

When you act from non-attachment, you do not carry the action as a perception of your mind. You set it free to last forever outside of your limited existence as a self. Your mind brands actions with values as being good or bad, with time and space. In the flow of reality, all actions dwell in a moment and once they are manifested, they are perfect as they are.

Is manifestation not just the end result of an action, conscious or not? Even thinking is an action.

Manifestation is a clear appearance, an indication of existence.

Everything is a manifestation. An action can be a manifestation of a thought, thought can be a manifestation of chemical processes in our body, the body can be a manifestation of the elements, etc. Only in our physical eyes do actions have beginnings and endings. Actions may be revealed when there is an observer, but they are *constantly* constant in existence.

When the Tao Te Ching says, "When nothing is done, nothing is left undone," it means you should not approach the action with the thought, 'I am doing'. When you start with the intent of doing, it means you see things as incomplete. You have an idea about reality (it is not done), an idea about the present (it should be done), an idea about the future (it will be done) and an idea about the past (it was done).

The correct idea is to be in the moment and allow the action to manifest itself or reveal itself through you, without disturbing the process by having the thought, 'I am doing'. A tree doesn't think, 'I am creating shade'. It simply manifests the shade, or it doesn't.

Is it alright to have goals?

Goals are part of our existence. Even when you decide to go to the washroom you are setting up a small goal to get there. There is nothing wrong with having goals.

The problem with goals starts when your goals are set up for the purpose of fulfilling the 'self's' definition of who you are.

The other negative part of having goals comes with expectations for specific results. If we do not achieve the results we expected, we experience disappointment. Disappointment is one source of our suffering.

For example, if part of your definition as a 'self' is being a mother/parent, you probably will get obsessed with fulfilling this role as a goal (I have to have 2, 3, 4 children). If you can't fulfill the goal of being a mother, you will feel that your identity is falling apart, and your 'self' is disappearing. This is when misery takes place.

Most of our life we chase after goals which will help us to complete the definition of who we *think* we are;

I am a parent, so my goal is to have children and be a good parent.

I am spiritual, so my goal is to be compassionate, to become realized.

I am a business man, so my goal is to do lots of deals, to be wealthy.

I am a lover, so my goal is to be admired, to give/get pleasure.

If your definition of yourself is "I am an educated person", no matter how many goals you set up to fulfill this definition, the small self will always be at risk. Maybe somebody will be more educated than you, or maybe somebody won't acknowledge your education etc. This is where suffering arises.

The stress that individuals are experiencing in modern society is a result of running like mice after goals that will help them to be 'somebody'. If people fail to achieve their goals, their small self suffers from an inability to fulfill their definition. If they are successful in fulfilling their goals they will constantly worry about losing what they have gained (love, money, status, stability). This is the trap of fulfilling your self-definition.

More and more, young people study things that they don't have any real interest in, because their goal is to be 'successful'.

People work in jobs they don't like because their goal is to be rich.

People think that they are making their own authentic choices in life, but most of the time they act without choice, as they attempt to fulfill the desire of their small self to be 'somebody'. Some people, (after years of trying to fulfill their goals), wake up to the realization that what they are doing and what they have achieved does not actually fulfill their true nature. This is the essence of what is commonly known as a 'mid life crisis'.

It is fine to have a goal to go for a vacation, and it is fine to plan it the best you can to manifest it, but what if you face an airline strike on the day of travel? You may never get to your destination. The question is, as a result, are you in pain, or are you at ease?

Why do people often perceive the same moment or event differently? While one gains joy, the other may experience pain from the same moment.

The answer is that each of us experiences 'parallel realities'.

An old story tells of a Zen master, while walking every morning to the monastery, who saw an old woman standing in the corner of the street weeping. One day, curious, he walked to the woman and asked her why it was that, no matter what the weather, she stood there crying?

The old woman replied, "I have two daughters and they are both happily married to merchants. One is married to an umbrella shop owner, and the other is married to a sandal shop owner. On rainy days I cry for the one who has a sandal shop, knowing that no one will buy sandals in the rain. On sunny days I weep for the one who owns the umbrella shop, knowing that no one will buy an umbrella on a sunny day."

The master said, "Why not, for a change, on a sunny day be happy for the one who sells sandals, and on the rainy days be happy for the one who sells umbrellas?"

We all live in two realities that run simultaneously in parallel lines, and they seldom meet. One is the reality that happens as an objective event, and the other is the reality that occurs in our subjective mind as a result of the way we perceived the event.

Here's a scenario. "She entered the store with her

expensive clothes, looking at me from above as though I was a 'nobody'. I felt intimated by her." This is the first reality, which is the one most illusionary.

What actually happened was that a woman entered the store wearing clothes, with her eyes open. The rest of the description and feelings happened in the mind of the observer. This is the second reality.

We hang on to the two realities, in the same way that an acrobat swings between two bars. We swing from one reality to the other, with no grounding under our feet for clarity, and no idea of what is real and what is not.

In the motion of the swinging, we produce endless emotions that, most of the time, are not relevant to the moment. Rarely do we face reality 'as it is', without any commentary from the mind.

Another scenario:

It's *raining,* so I am excited to spend a romantic evening with my beloved.

It's *raining,* so I feel very lonely and depressed.

It's *raining,* is the same in both realities. The interpretation of the *actuality* (it is romantic, it is depressing) is the fiction that happens in the mind.

The diversity of emotions we feel through life arises from the reality we form in the mind about 'the experience'.

Add E – for ego – before motion (a pure action) and you get e-motion. Ego triggered by action.

Emotion comes from the Latin word *emovere* which means to stir up, agitate or excite.

Unlike the observer who experiences the motion objectively (she is walking into the store), the ego will stir up its own interpretation of the observed motion ('she looks superior') and will create an (e)motion: ('I feel intimated').

Another simple example: imagine a couple, dancing together on the dance floor.

This is one of the parallel realities, one which actually happens in a real moment.

An older woman sitting close to the dancing couple feels joy watching their wonderful performance, which reminds her of her youth. This is the other parallel reality, one that doesn't actually happen on the dance floor but only in the old woman's mind. The mind blends its own association into the observed action, and creates an e-motion, in this case, *joy*.

On the contrary, if it's your girlfriend dancing with another man you may feel *jealousy* and *anger*. Those emotions don't happen on the dance floor either, but only in the mind.

Being the observer, moving through experiences with no attachment, judgment or personal interpretation is a consequence of seeing reality as it is: just *"two people dancing together on the dance floor."*

In the same way that projective theories of geometry[1] predict that two parallel lines might possibly meet at infinity, our parallel realities unite beyond time and space. The unity occurs when the mind disappears and a true experience takes place. In this moment we shift from emotional swings to a state of ease.

---

1 Projective geometry – The branch of geometry dealing with the properties and invariants of geometric figures under projection. In older literature, projective geometry is sometimes called "higher geometry."

The End

The End

When you write a book, how do you know when the book ends? I guess the same question can be asked about life as well. When you live life, how do you know when life ends? Many people's lives end long *before* their hearts stop beating, while others' lives continue long *after* their hearts stop beating. Life starts, and ends in one moment, so, if you are in the moment, you will know!

Sources

The Concise Oxford Dictionary, Oxford University Press, New York, 8th edition

Oxford Paperback Dictionary Thesaurus, Oxford University Press, New York, 2001

Dictionary definitions not otherwise remarked are from the *Visual Thesaurus, (http://visualthesaurus. com),* Copyright (c)1998-2007 Thinkmap, Inc. All rights reserved

The Power of Myth, Joseph Campbell, Doubleday Books, 1988

About the Author

About the Author

After nearly 30 years of personal practice and teaching thousands of students around the globe, shakti mhi has made Zen, meditation and yoga her passion and her life's purpose. Since the age of 14 when she first discovered the transformative power of meditation, she has journeyed around the world in search of teaching to deepen her knowledge. Her exploration of the ancient ways of connecting with the inner self also led her to study Zen, clarifying her understanding of the original intent of Yoga. From living at a Yoga ashram in India, to spending a year in contemplation in a middle-eastern desert, she has completely dedicated her life to study and teaching. Never satisfied with the status quo, she has always insisted on questioning all beliefs, opting instead for the authentic personal experience. She instills the same attitude of experiential self-discovery in all her students.

shakti is the founder of Prana Yoga Teacher College, which is Canada's first and only fully accredited college of yoga, attracting students from around the world. Since 1982, she has trained hundreds of Yoga teachers, who are sought after by yoga studios and practitioners around the world. Many of them have gone on to open their own schools internationally. Teacher training courses and retreats are offered in Canada, Thailand, China, Israel, Mexico and Europe. Much of the appeal of her teaching comes from the unique style she has developed over the years. The signature of her practice is the integration of breath control and the intuitive flow of the asanas, creation and retention of prana (Sanskrit, for life-force) while stilling the mind into a meditative enjoyment of the present moment.

Shakti is also the author of a bestselling instructional DVD, "The Yoga Experience".

For more information about shakti and her teaching schedule please visit www.pranayogacollege.com

NOTES FOR CONTEMPLATION

NOTES FOR CONTEMPLATION